The Scribbler

by George Mendoza

illustrated by Robert Quackenbush

HOLT, RINEHART & WINSTON, INC.
New York Chicago San Francisco

About the author:

George Mendoza is one of the most diversified and prolific of today's writers for children. With more than forty books to his credit, he has been characterized by one reviewer as, "a most unpredictable young man, an original and independent talent." A native New Yorker and Columbia graduate, he lives in Manhattan with his wife and small daughter, though the family frequently retreats to southern Vermont.

About the artist:

Robert Quackenbush lives in New York City, where he is a painter, teacher, designer, and illustrator. The artist for more than fifty books for children and adults, his work has been exhibited in leading museums throughout the country. To illustrate *The Scribbler,* he took the work to Trinidad Bay in the heart of northern California's redwood country. All the scenes were drawn on location there.

About the book:

The text and display have been hand-lettered by the artist and the illustrations were rendered with colored inks and pen line. The book is printed by offset.

•

for Alice Miller...full moon rising...d.m.
and for all the children at Moonstone...r.q.

Across the blue-green feathered sea
come waves crashing on the shore,
curling in the eye
like flowers flowing,
white clover bursting in the spray.

But the sandpiper shows he couldn't care.

He is a scribbler.

All day he twit-twits
up the beach, down the beach,
scribbling on the sand.

Sea spiders on stilts of bony legs
can't seem to make up their minds
to stay or leave their little holes
that fall away into the mole-dark clay.

But the sandpiper races in and out of waves.

He is a scribbler.

All day he twit-twits

up the beach, down the beach,

scribbling on the sand.

Shells are sailing up to shore
where sailors disembark from silver spirals,
songs that held the rudder strong
sift through a sea of dune-flutes.

But the sandpiper flicks his feathers dry.

He is a scribbler.

All day he twit-twits

up the beach, down the beach,

scribbling on the sand.

A minnow-plane
darts into a parachute of cloud
pinwheeling down the sky—
a piece of bait
tied to a dreamstring.

But the sandpiper never lifts his head.

He is a scribbler.

All day he twit-twits

up the beach, down the beach,

scribbling on the sand.

Children fill up plastic buckets
from the five-and-dime
with scoops of sand and dreams.
It's not so far to dig a hole
to take you out the other side.

But the sandpiper pecks the ground to eat.
He is a scribbler.
All day he twit-twits
up the beach, down the beach,
scribbling on the sand.

A baby sleeps
in the spills of shadows
cast by droopy purple flowers
climbing out of castles in the air.

But the sandpiper chases a dream in the sandy drift.

He is a scribbler.

All day he twit-twits

up the beach, down the beach,

scribbling on the sand.

An old man
walks along the edge of shore.
His head is down, his back is bent,
his time to trace the lonely lace
thrown up by ancient waves
hissing back into the ground.

But the sandpiper frolics in the foam.
He is a scribbler.
All day he twit-twits
up the beach, down the beach,
scribbling on the sand.

A boy
pressing his ear
against the ocean's splashing mat
listens to a tune from the tide
coming through the rock-shell crush of land.

But the sandpiper hears only the hum of the wind.

He is a scribbler.

All day he twit-twits

up the beach, down the beach,

scribbling on the sand.

Turn the world over,
skim across poppy petals of light.
You'll ride a cockleshell boat
down the rivers of a rainbow.

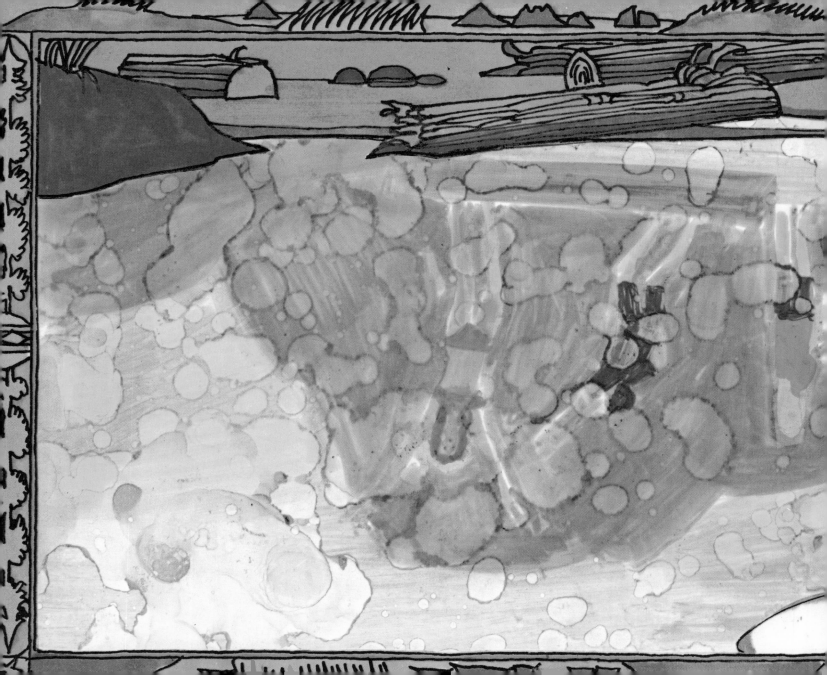

But the sandpiper struts and bobs.

He is a scribbler.

All day he twit-twits

up the beach, down the beach,

scribbling on the sand.

The sun dips down
as a flower folds.
Night is coming
like a stranger on the trail.

But the sandpiper
is tucked like a leaf
in the cooling brush,
scribbling on the walls of sleep.